YOU CAN DRAW FANTASY FIGURES
DRAWING
DUNGEON CREATURES

BY STEVE SIMS

Gareth Stevens
Publishing

Please visit our Web site, www.garethstevens.com. For a free color catalog of all our high-quality books, call toll free 1-800-542-2595 or fax 1-877-542-2596.

Library of Congress Cataloging-in-Publication Data

Sims, Steve (Steve P.), 1980-
Drawing dungeon creatures / Steve Sims.
    p. cm. – (You can draw fantasy figures)
Includes index.
ISBN 978-1-4339-4058-3 (library binding)
ISBN 978-1-4339-4059-0 (pbk.)
ISBN 978-1-4339-4060-6 (6-pack)
1. Fantasy in art–Juvenile literature. 2. Drawing–Technique–Juvenile literature. I. Title.
NC825.F25S56 2011
743'.87–dc22

                              2010013015

First Edition

Published in 2011 by
Gareth Stevens Publishing
111 East 14th Street, Suite 349
New York, NY 10003

Copyright © 2011 Arcturus Publishing

Artwork and Text: Steve Sims
Editors: Kate Overy and Joe Harris
Designer: Steve Flight

Printed in the United States of America

CPSIA compliance information: Batch #AS10GS: For further information contact Gareth Stevens, New York, New York at 1-800-542-2595.

SL001639US

CONTENTS

Drawing and Inking Tips

In the world of swords and sorcery, heroes can perform extraordinary feats of valor that would be impossible in the real world. However, it's still essential that your characters should look solid and believable. So here are some helpful hints to keep in mind.

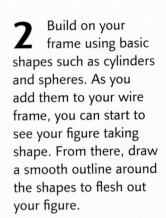

1 First, work out your character's posture and attitude using a wire frame. You can look in the mirror to work out how a pose might work!

2 Build on your frame using basic shapes such as cylinders and spheres. As you add them to your wire frame, you can start to see your figure taking shape. From there, draw a smooth outline around the shapes to flesh out your figure.

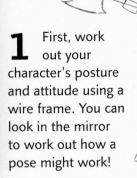

TOP TIP!

Most adult human figures are seven times the height of their head. Draw your character's head, then calculate his or her height by measuring three heads for the legs, one for the lower torso, and two for the upper body.

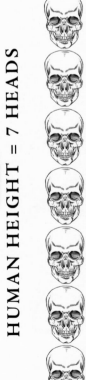

HUMAN HEIGHT = 7 HEADS

3 When things are looking good and your character is complete, you can start to ink the picture. Inking allows us to choose the best lines we have drawn in pencil and make them stand out from the rest.

Coloring Tips

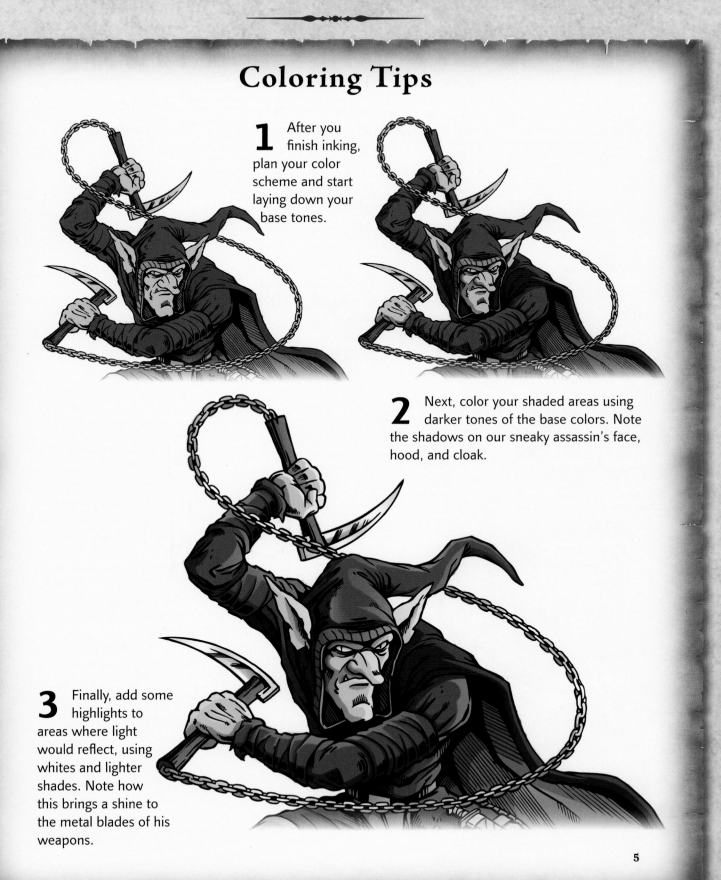

1 After you finish inking, plan your color scheme and start laying down your base tones.

2 Next, color your shaded areas using darker tones of the base colors. Note the shadows on our sneaky assassin's face, hood, and cloak.

3 Finally, add some highlights to areas where light would reflect, using whites and lighter shades. Note how this brings a shine to the metal blades of his weapons.

ORC WARRIOR

The orcs form an impenetrable wall of pure power and brutality, making them an evil army's deadliest weapons. Brandishing fierce weapons, they march into battle with an unstoppable fury, allowing nothing to stand in their way.

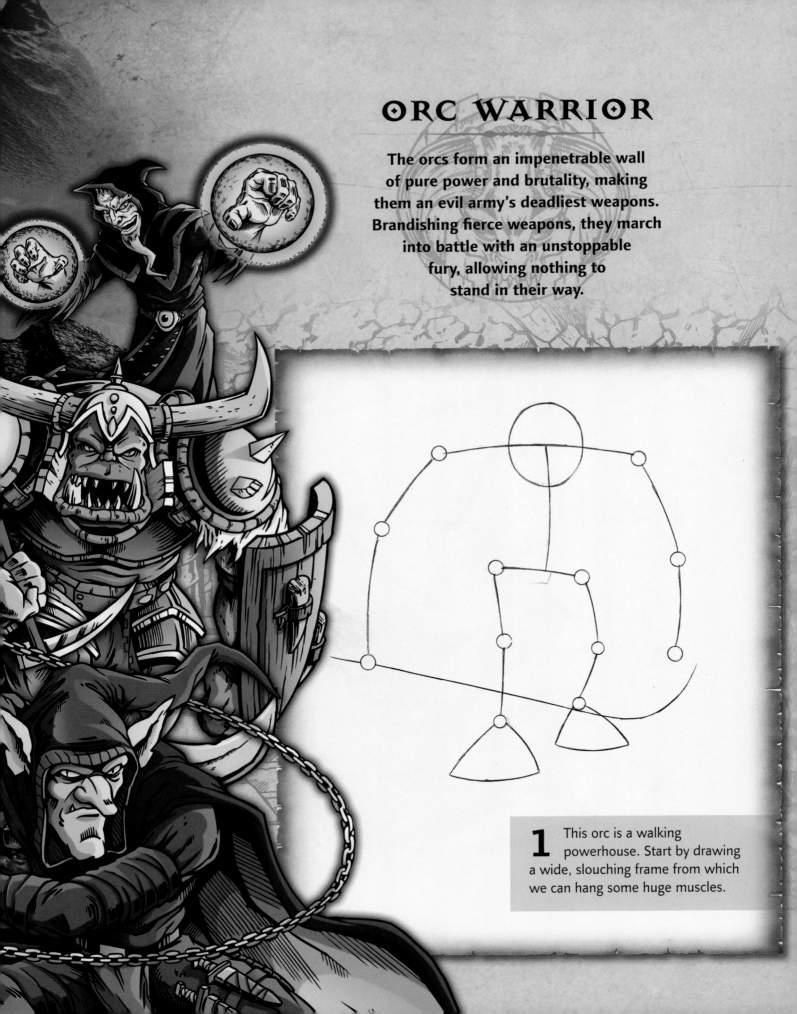

1 This orc is a walking powerhouse. Start by drawing a wide, slouching frame from which we can hang some huge muscles.

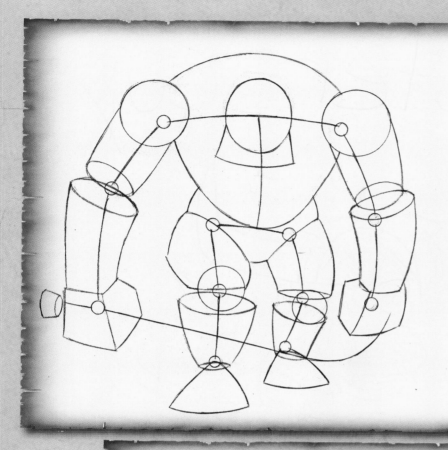

2 Build his body using basic shapes, but remember to make his chest, shoulders, and arms bigger than those of a normal man—this is one big guy!

3 Once you have the basic outline in place, remove your frame and construction shapes. Now it's time to develop specific areas of interest, namely the orc's big, muscular arms, the horns that protrude through his helmet, and his big, lumbering feet. Also pencil in his shield and sword.

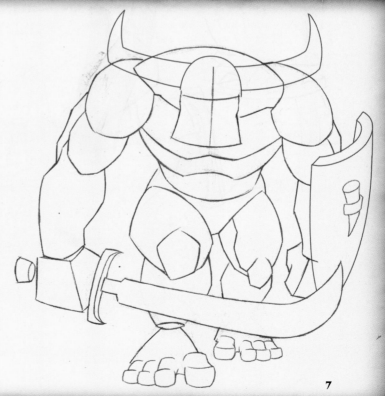

7

4 Add in your orc's helmet, chest plate, shoulder guards, and cuff. Pencil in his face, remembering that orcs have mainly small features and beady eyes, but big, powerful jaws and teeth. This brute has a broken tooth from a battle.

TOP TIP !

Add horns, spikes, and extra pointy bits to make sure your characters' armor looks as intimidating as their weapons.

5 Now it's time to make your orc look really tough by adding all of your final details. An orc's purpose in life is to fight, so focus on his armor and weapon. Torn clothing, scars, and a cracked toenail will give him a battle-worn look.

6 Now it's time to ink your character. Heavy inking works well for orcs, as it adds to their brutality. Try not to lose any of the details in his armor.

ORC WARRIOR

7 Once you're happy with the inking, it's time to add color to your character. Muted, earthy colors are the best choice for orcs. Use a dull gray for his body armor and a sandy brown for his skin.

GOBLIN ASSASSIN

The goblin assassin is an evil, calculating
character who hides in the shadows
waiting for the moment to deliver a fatal
attack. Hardly noticeable within the chaos
of the battlefield, he only reveals himself
to his victim as he delivers
a deadly strike.

1 It's time to tackle
the sneakiest goblin
of them all. Start with
your usual wire frame,
drawing the character in
a crouching pose with
one leg outstretched.
Our character should be
crouching low and ready
to strike at any moment.

GOBLIN ASSASSIN

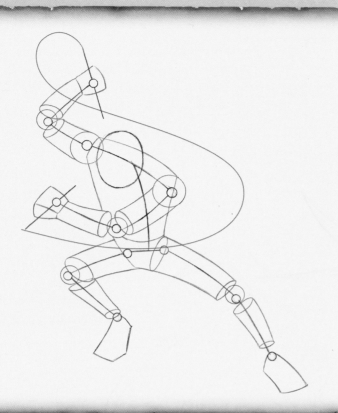

2 Fill out the frame with the basic shapes and add the swooping line of the assassin's chain.

3 Draw your figure around the construction shapes. When you're happy with how he's looking, erase the construction lines from step 2. Note the long, pointed shape of the goblin's head and ears. Draw the long, flowing shape of his hat and the outline of his weapons.

4 Pencil in his cloak, boots, and facial features. Make the line that joins his two scythes (weapons) wide enough to add in the chain detail in the next step. Remember to add the trademark goblin nose!

TOP TIP !

Small, beady eyes and a mean, furrowed brow help to demonstrate the nasty nature of this character.

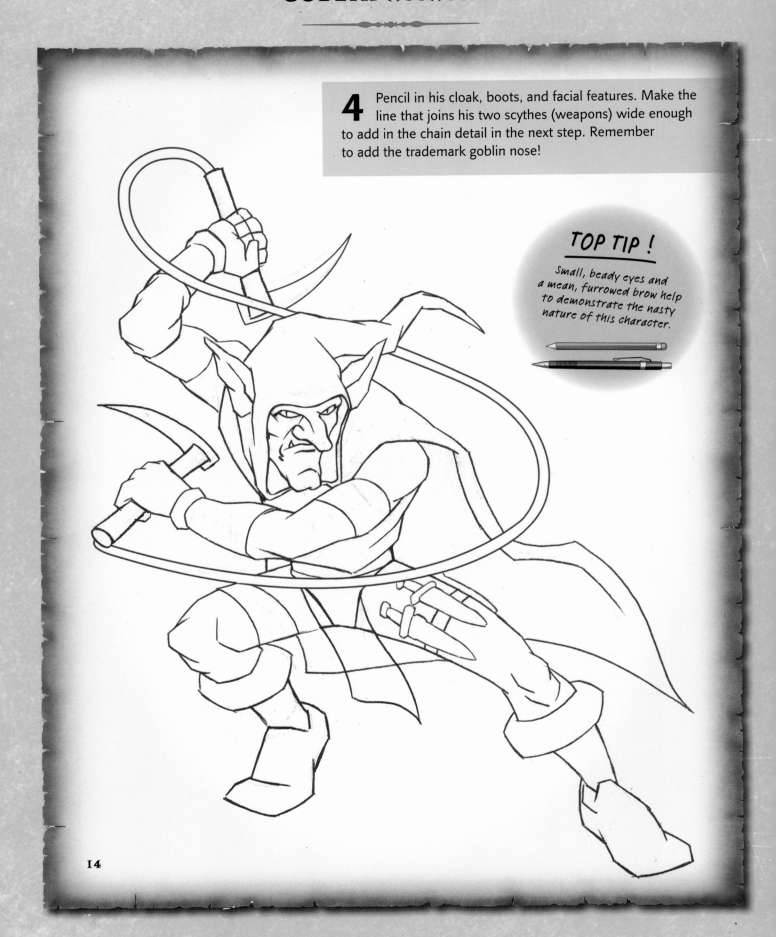

5 Now add all the final details. Pay attention to the chain joining his weapons. Take your time and draw the links one after the other. Use the lines you have drawn in step 4 to guide the path of the chain.

6 When you're inking your goblin, add a good amount of shading to the underside of his cloak and inside his hood. Fill in the center of each link in the chain, too.

7 Finally, add some color. Your assassin needs to blend with his surroundings, so greens and browns are good colors for his clothes. Don't forget his bright green goblin skin and glowing yellow eyes.

EVIL WIZARD

Practicing the dark arts for hundreds of years has taken its toll on this evil wizard's physical appearance. However, he has built up immense magical powers and the ability to wield the deadliest of dark spells.

1 We want our wizard to have an air of mystery about him, so we're going to draw him floating in midair. Use a curve for the continuation of his body to the point where his legs would end. Draw two large circles over his hands as a base for his magic orbs.

3 Add some basic detail and start to remove your construction shapes. Give the figure a smooth, flowing lower body. Give the bottom of his robe a ragged edge and draw the outline of the hood.

2 Fill in the basic shapes using a curved, bendy rectangle as an outline for the robe.

19

4 Once you're happy with your pencil outline, give your wizard wild eyebrows, a crooked beard, and a wicked glare. Add the flowing detail at his waist and give his sleeves the same ragged outline as the bottom of his robe. Draw the curling fingers on his hands.

TOP TIP !

Use short, sharp lines to make the edge of the robe look shaggy and ragged. Don't worry about joining all the lines, as the gaps will add to the effect.

5 Keep adding detail to your wizard. Concentrate on his robe, adding lots of shading to indicate folds in the material, and draw an evil eye decoration on his belt. Use fine dashes inside the magical orbs that surround his hands to create a hazy effect.

6 Use a light inking technique so that you keep all the fine detail from the final pencil stage. Only add thicker, solid ink to areas such as the folds in the fabric where we need depth. Be very delicate with the outer circles of the magical orbs.

7 Dark blue robes will give your wizard a mysterious, malevolent quality. Use a bright green for his magical orbs to give them a glowing, unearthly feel. Note how some of the green glow has illuminated his face and robe.

The Dungeon

Now that you've mastered how to draw three different types of characters, it's time to create a setting where our dungeon creatures can lurk while they hatch their diabolical plans. Imagine an eerily lit underground den, full of traps and snares to capture any unwary adventurers who might venture inside in search of treasure.

1 Start by drawing a horizon line across the page and adding straight perspective lines. These will help you to work out the right angles for objects, which will give the dungeon a sense of depth. You'll notice that in this scene our vanishing point—the point where the perspective lines would meet—is off to the side of the paper. It just happens to fall out of the area we are concentrating on.

2 Once the basic shapes of your room are blocked in using your perspective lines as a guide, you can start to add extra ghastly elements to decorate your dungeon. How about a skeleton hanging from the wall, as a warning to univited guests?

3 With the basic structures in place, you can continue to flesh out your deadly dungeon with as many disgusting details as you like! Tentacles, torches, and skulls are always a good place to start. You can give the room a gothic feel by adding claws and skulls to the walls and doorways, too.

4 Now it's time to concentrate on textures. You'll notice that we've added a slick, slimy substance oozing out of the hollows on the walls, and dripping from the tentacles. The look of the rocky walls is created by drawing rough, incomplete shapes like broken circles. Patches of shading on the floor make it look bumpy and uneven.

25

5 Now apply the ink, adding darker contrasting areas to the shadows. Be careful not to go overboard with the black areas, or your image may end up looking a little bit flat.

6 Remember when coloring a scene like this that the secondary colors—purple, green, and orange—are great for creating a weird, creepy feel. Also notice how the sinister glow of the torches and the wizard's magical orbs are reflected in the stone arches and the door frame.

Adventurers' Armory

Heroes' weapons are made with fair play in mind. They rely on the skill of the wielder to win the day, rather than foul play or sneaky attacks. Weapons created for good are made from wood, leather, and pure metals.

SOLDIER'S SPEAR

A long and sturdy weapon. Ideal to use when charging at the enemy.

HAMMER

Most often used by dwarves. Made from stone chiseled from the depths of the mountains where they dwell.

WOODEN SHIELD

Adorned with a dragon's eye to give protection against evil during battle.

WARRIOR'S SWORD

A straight and trusty blade, often decorated with runes or jewels.

ELVEN BOW

Carved from the boughs of trees that grow in the enchanted forests where the elves make their home.

Wicked Weaponry

These deadly weapons are designed to wreak havoc and destruction. They are used by corrupt, evil warriors, and are often enchanted with curses or dark magic to cause plagues and devastation with every blow.

SHAMAN'S STAFF

A fiery scepter used to conjure up all kinds of evil.

DEMON AXE

A mighty and fearful axe wielded by the wickedest warriors and charged with the blackest of magic for extra power.

ORC'S BLADE

A huge and deadly sword decorated with a spiked skull and made from cursed metals.

DEADLY DAGGER

A twisted and torturous blade with sharp hand guards and a jagged blade for tearing flesh. It is also infused with a plague that will slowly poison and kill its victim.

EVIL SHIELD

Decorated with a malevolent face to strike fear in the hearts of enemies.

ASSASSIN'S SICKLE

This is as deadly and sneaky as the warrior who wields it.

31

Glossary

brandish wave around in a threatening way
brutality viciousness and cruelty
furrowed marked with deep lines or wrinkles
highlights the lightest colored parts of an image
illuminate make bright
impenetrable impossible to pass through
intimidating frightening
malevolent wanting evil things to happen
muted soft and calm
orb sphere
perspective a way of drawing that makes objects look three-dimensional
posture the position of someone's body
scepter a royal staff
scythe a bladed staff, usually used for cutting crops
sturdy tough and strong
texture the way the surface of an object looks or feels
valor courage in battle
vanishing point the place where perspective lines appear to come together into a point

Further Reading

Cowan, Finlay. *Drawing and Painting Fantasy Figures: From the Imagination to the Page*. London: David and Charles, 2004.
Hart, Christopher. *How to Draw Fantasy Characters*. New York: Watson-Guptill, 1999.
Renaigle, Damon J. *Draw Medieval Fantasies*. Cincinnati, OH: Peel Productions, 1995.

Index